What Kind
of House
Are You?

What Kind of House Are You?

CALVIN H. TAYLOR

ARPress
ILLUMINATING IDEAS,
EMPOWERING VOICES

ARPress

45 Dan Road Suite 5

Canton, MA 02021

Hotline: 1(888) 821-0229

Fax: 1(508) 545-7580

Ordering Information:

Quantity sales. Special discounts are available on quantity purchases by corporations, associations, and others. For details, contact the publisher at the address above.

Printed in the United States of America.

ISBN-13:   Softcover   979-8-89356-244-6
              eBook   979-8-89356-245-3

Library of Congress Control Number: 2024911990

TABLE OF CONTENTS

INTRODUCTION

We as people don't take time to consider what God went to create us. He first made us a home to live in then created us from the dust of the ground, blew the breath of life into us, and we became living being. One who is three parts—being, body, soul, and spirit—and then given dominion over all that was created by his hand.

One Thursday night after Bible study, Pastor Vincent Winfrey asked me to teach Bible study for several weeks to the membership of Freedom Church International. I began to seek the lord as to what I should teach, and so while meditating, I heard the question asked, *What kind of house are you?* Although the question asked give the impression of a physical house, the true point is what type of spiritual house are you. *I have learned that the most complicated problem had already been broken down to the simplest answer.* One of the many lessons taught by the Holy Spirit.

After hearing that question being asked of me, I didn't have an answer. The Holy Spirit brought to mind how the Lord chose a place in time and created the heaven and the earth. In the space of the five days. God, Holy Spirit, and the Word created the day and night, separated the waters that was above—heaven, denoting "sky"—from the waters that were below. Then it caused those waters that were below to be pooled into one place and dry land appeared. The dry land God called earth and the waters moving into one place, seas. God command the earth to bring forth grass and herbs, yielding seeds after their type, and trees yielding fruit after each type, whose seeds are in the fruit, thereby seeding the earth. God then made the sun, moon, and stars to separate the day from the night. The stars and moon rule the night and the sun, the day, and they were given for signs, for seasons, for days, and for years.

The Lord said to the waters in the earth to bring forth abundantly every moving creature ("whales and great fish large and small after their kind"), fowl that fly in the sky after their kind. Now on the fifth day, the Lord command the earth to bring forth every living creature after their kind, every creeping thing after their kind, and beasts of the earth after their kind. Now that the house was done, the Lord desired a representation of himself to be the occupant of this house. On the sixth day, the Lord made man, both male and female, he created them and gave them power and authority over all that was created. The Lord saw all that has been done was good, so he rested on the seventh day. God had made a home for man to dwell in and to rule from and to have a relationship with him. The Psalmist says it so beautifully in Psalm 8:4–9,

> What is man, that you are mindful of him? And the son of man, that you visit him? For you have made him a little lower than the angels, and have crowned him with glory and honor. You made him to have dominion over the works of your hands; you have put all things under his feet: All sheep and oxen, yea, and the beasts of the field; The fowl of the air, and the fish of the sea, and whatsoever passes through the paths of the seas. O Lord our Lord, how excellent is your name in all the earth!

I heard the spirit of the Lord say, "He made a home for you." Then the question was asked of me, "How would you have done it?" There was no hesitation in my spirit, I began to think about the steps that would be taken to do as the Spirit had asked. Building a house or a temple that God could dwell in. "Know ye not that you are the temple of God, and that the spirit of God dwelleth in you" (1 Corinthians 3:16). When we think about how our spiritual life is made up, we then can liken it to building of a house.

STEP 1

Making the Ground Ready
for the Foundation

The preaching of the Gospel of Jesus Christ. For in the Scripture, it says:

> How then shall they call on him in whom they have not believed? and how shall they believe in him of whom they have not heard? and how shall they hear without a preacher? And how shall they preach, except they be sent? as it is written, how beautiful are the feet of them that preach the gospel of peace, and bring glad tidings of good things! So, then faith comes by hearing, and hearing by the word of God. (Roman 10:14–15, 17)

So we see the importance of witnessing, for no one can save him or herself but only through the salvation of Jesus Christ.

In hearing the salvation story, we are made to know that "God so loved the world that he gave his only begotten Son, that whosoever believeth in him should not perish, but have everlasting life" (John 3:16). "Whereby the disobedience of one man [Adam], sin entered in the world and so death was passed on to all men, for all have sinned"

(Roman 5:12). Therefore, the lost must believe that Jesus Christ came into being to show us God's love, to be a sacrifice for our sin, rose on the third day according to Scripture, and now resides on the right hand of God as our intercessor. The lost cannot believe until they have heard the good news of salvation, cannot hear the salvation story without a witness, and that witness must be filled with the spirit of Christ Jesus walking there in building up the faith as we have been taught and increasing in faith and thanksgiving (Colossians 2:6–7).

STEP 2

Laying the Foundation: Jesus Christ

After the good news of salvation has been given unto the lost and they realized that they are lost without a savior, who is Jesus Christ, and they believe that he able to save confession is uttered, Romans 10:9–10 tells us:

> That if you shall confess with your mouth the Lord Jesus, and shall believe in your heart that God has raised him from the dead, you shall be saved. For with the heart man believes unto righteousness; and with the mouth confession is made unto salvation.

This is the promise that God has given unto us. Jesus said that he was the door by which if any man would be saved, he may go in and out of the presence of God and have an answer for any situation through God's word.

"For other foundation can no man lay than that is laid, which is Jesus Christ," (1 Corinthians 3:11). Nothing else can substitute for Jesus Christ being our savior. The results of our confession of faith in Jesus Christ is a new birth happening; "therefore, if any man be in Christ, he is a new creature: old things are passed away; behold, all things are become new. And all things are of God, who has reconciled us to himself by Jesus Christ, and has given to us the ministry of reconciliation" (2 Corinthians 5:17, 18), and God so empower us to witness to the lost about what that saving power has done in us and that same saving grace can be done in them through the faith in his Son, Jesus Christ. Second Corinthians 5:21 says, "For he has made him [Jesus] to be sin for us, who knew no sin; that we might be made the righteousness of God in him." No self-righteousness, nor good works, self-rehabilitation, or trying to justify oneself through the law. "For by grace are all of you saved through faith; and that not of yourselves: it is the gift of God" (Ephesians 2:8).

STEP 3

The Frame: Faith

Faith is a result of step 1 and 2 and is the framework of which everything is built upon the foundation. Hebrews 11:1 answers the question of what faith is: "Now faith is the substance of things hoped for, the evidence of things not seen." We who are alive today having not seen the Lord Jesus Christ, yet we believe that he is our Savior. The Bible tells us in Isaiah 55:6, "Seek you the Lord while he may be found, call you upon him while he is near," and Matthew 7:7 says, "Ask, and it shall be given you; seek, and you shall find; knock, and it shall be opened unto you." It is the desire to know the Lord Jesus Christ that will cause us to seek him in spirit, to ask him to teach us how to live a godly life and know the height, depth, and width of his love so that we may show that same love to our fellowmen.

As the Lord affirms all that we have heard of him, our eyes of understanding of him is increased, and he makes it known what is the hope of his calling (which was and is to redeem us from sin), and what the riches of the glory of his inheritance in the saints (the restoration of us all back into the family of God). Therefore, we who have been called out of darkness (because we did not know the Lord) should show forth praise unto the lord who has called us out of unknowing into his marvelous light of knowing him. He has called us a chosen generation, a royal priesthood, a holy nation, and exclusive people. "Blessed is the man that trusts in the Lord and whose hope the Lord is. For he shall be as a tree planted by the waters and that spreads out her roots by the river, and shall not see when heat comes, but her leaf shall be green; shall not be careful in the year of drought, neither shall cease from yielding fruits" (Jeremiah 17:7–8). *Faith* as a yielding fruit becomes the *drapes or curtains* of our *heart*, because it causes us to reach for peace:

> If it be possible, as much as lies in you, live peaceably with all men. (Roman 12:18)

STEP 4

The Walls: Holy Spirit

Surely if faith is our frame, then the Holy Spirit is the wall that gives our building its shape and appeal. Jesus informing his disciples that his mission here on earth was coming to an end said unto them:

> Nevertheless, I tell you the truth; It is expedient for you that I go away: for if I go not away, the Comforter will not come unto you; but if I depart, I will send him unto you. Nevertheless, when he, the Spirit of truth, has come, he will guide you into all truth: for he shall not speak of himself; but whatsoever he shall hear, that shall he speak: and he will show you things to come. He shall glorify me: for he shall receive of mine, and shall show it unto you. (John 16:7, 13–14)

> But the Comforter, which is the Holy Spirit, whom the Father will send in my name, he shall teach you all things, and bring all things to your remembrance, whatsoever I have said unto you. (John 14:26)

Hereby we know that we walk with the Lord because of the Holy Spirit being that true witness of and for the Lord Jesus Christ. Jesus said in Acts 1:8 that all of us "shall receive power after the Holy Spirit has come upon us and we shall be witnesses of the Lord's both in Jerusalem, and in all Judaea, and in Samaria, and unto the uttermost part of the earth." "And these signs shall follow them that believe; In my name shall they cast out devils; they shall speak with new tongues" (Mark 16:17).

STEP 5

Roof: God

When we think about the roof, it is the most important part of the building, for it covers and keeps the health of the house. When the roof leaks, the house begins to rot. God is our roof, and he wants us to known him, and the more we know him, the better our covering. God is known by many names, but the one name he gave himself was I Am, the everlasting God, the one true God with no beginning and no end (Exodus 3:14).

He is a present help in the time of trouble. David praised God in Psalm 139:7–10,

> Where shall I go from your spirit? or where shall I flee from your presence? If I ascend up into heaven, you are there: if I make my bed in hell, behold, you are there. If I take the wings of the morning, and dwell in the uttermost parts of the sea; Even there shall your hand lead me, and your right hand shall hold me,

For he acknowledges that God was and everlasting God, a merciful God and a covenant keeping God.

Yes, the roof covers the whole house, and God wants you to know that he can cover all of us and his various name reflects that caring and nature of him. When we as children learn who the father is, we begin to know him by his names: *El Elyon*, "the Exalted One" or "God Most High," the creator-owner of both heaven and earth; *El Shadday*, the covenant-making God and a God who is *all-powerful and all-sufficient* to provide; *Jehovah Jireh*, the Lord that sees and who provides and thereby makes it easy to cast all our cares upon him, for he cares for us.

STEP 6

Steps and Porch: Desiring a Relationship with God

In order to enter into the presence of God and to know him, Matthew 7:7–8 states: "Ask, and it shall be given you; seek, and you shall find; knock and it shall be open unto you: For every one that asked receives; and he who seeks finds; and to him that knocks it shall be open unto him." Ask, seek, and knock are our steps to bring us into a relationship with God, and prayer is the porch by which we receive that which we have ask for, the love of God which sought and the understanding of the breath of God.

Prayer is that integral part that is required for and in the relationship with God. Our confidence in God is made strong in him. When we have a need, whether spiritual or physical, we go to him and ask according to his will, we know that our request will be acted upon (ask, receive) (1 John 5:14,15).

When we have a need and we go to God in prayer—that is the knocking—yet the doors of heaven just don't seem to be opening, know that the will of God is to bless you. Continue to seek the unrevealed will of God until that which unseen is seen and the doors are opened—that is, knocking until the finding. God shows us how consistent he is in his love for us through Matthew 7:9–11, for it's says that if our children would come to us and ask for a piece of break would we give them a stone, or they ask for a fish would we give them a snake? If we then being evil know how to give good gifts unto our children, how much more shall our Father, which in heavens give good gifts to them that ask.

STEP 7

Windows: Sound Understanding

The beauty of a house is not only the location of where it is seated or the warmth of its inside; it is also the view from the inside to the outside. Proverbs 2:1–12 says,

My son, if you will receive my words, and hide my commandments with you; So that you incline your ear unto wisdom, and apply your heart to understanding; Yea, if you cry after knowledge, and lift up your voice for understanding; If you seek her as silver, and search for her as for hid treasures; Then shall you understand the fear of the Lord, and find the knowledge of God. For the Lord gives wisdom: out of his mouth comes knowledge and understanding. He lays up sound wisdom for the righteous: he is a buckler to them that walk uprightly. He keeps the paths of judgment, and preserves the way of his saints. Then shall you understand righteousness, and judgment, and equity; yea, every good path. When wisdom enters into your heart, and knowledge is pleasant unto your soul; Discretion shall preserve you; understanding shall keep you: To deliver you from the way of the evil man, from the man that speaks perverse things.

Proverbs 3:1–13, says it again in this way:

> My son, forget not my law; but let your heart keep my commandments: For length of days, and long life, and peace, shall they add to you. Let not mercy and truth forsake you: bind them about your neck; write them upon the table of your heart: So, shall you find favor and good understanding in the sight of God and man. Trust in the Lord with all of your heart; and lean not unto your own understanding. In all your ways acknowledge him, and he shall direct your paths. Be not wise in your own eyes: fear the Lord, and depart from evil. It shall be health to your navel, and marrow to your bones.
>
> Honor the Lord with your substance, and with the first-fruits of all of your increase: So, shall your barns be filled with plenty, and your presses shall burst out with new wine. My son, despise not the chastening of the Lord; neither be weary of his correction: For whom the Lord loves he corrects; even as a father the son in whom he lights. Happy is the man that finds wisdom, and the man that gets understanding.

Seeing world in a new light from the security of your own place. It is in that same vein, as we increase in our relationship with God, we come to know him as *Abba* (our Father), our place in him and also the world.

STEP 8

Door: Jesus Christ

In any house, there may be many doors, but there one door that the family commits to using as primary entrance into the house. Unlike those types of houses, we have only one door by which we may enter into the presence of God and that is by his Son Jesus Christ. Jesus said in John 10:9–10, "I am the door: by me if any man enters in, he shall be saved, and shall go in and out, and find pasture. The thief comes not, but in order to steal, and to kill, and to destroy: I am come that they may have life and they might have it more abundantly"

Also in John 14:6–7: "Jesus says unto Phillip, I am the way, the truth, and the life: no man comes unto the Father, but by me. If all of you had known me, all of you should have known my Father also: and from henceforth all of you know him, and have seen him."

John 10:30 says, "Jesus and God the Father is one and that we are one with Jesus Christ and God the Father."

As our eyes of understanding become clear, we find that the only right way to seek and enter into the presence of God is by his Son Jesus Christ, for we truly recognize that Jesus died for us and now sited at the right hand of the father making intercession for us. We are his sheep, and he is our shepherd; where he leads, we will follow because he cares for us.

STEP 9

Fireplace: Love

A house become most appealing when a fireplace is position in a place where it beckons one to gather around. It presents a place of warmth, comfort, and strength; so, too, is love. Love is the greatest emotion that one could have; however, we must be aware that lust is the great imitator of love. Real love brings about the atmosphere an action of many things.

1. *Devotion. God's love toward us.* John 3:16 says, "For God so loved the world, that he gave his only begotten Son, that whosoever believes in him should not perish, but have everlasting life." Roman 8:31–33 says, "What shall we then say to these things? If God be for us, who can be against us? He that spared not his own Son, but delivered him up for us all, how shall he not with him also freely give us all things? Who shall lay anything to the charge of God's elect? It is God that justifies."

   Our love toward God. Roman 8:28 says, "And we know that all things work together for good to them that love God, to them who are the called according to his purpose."

   "I plead to you therefore, brethren, by the mercies of

God, that you present your bodies a living sacrifice, holy, acceptable unto God, which is your reasonable service. And be not conformed to this world: but be you transformed by the renewing of your mind, that all of you may prove what is that good, and acceptable, and perfect, will of God" (Roman 12:1–2).

2. *Strength.* "I can do all things through Christ which strengthens me" (Philippians 4:13).

3. *Power.* "But all of you shall receive power, after that the Holy Spirit has come upon you: and all of you shall be witnesses unto me both in Jerusalem, and in all Judaea, and in Samaria, and unto the uttermost part of the earth" (Acts 1:8).

"And these signs shall follow them that believe; In my name shall they cast out devils; they shall speak with new tongues; They shall take up serpents; and if they drink any deadly thing, it shall not hurt them; they shall lay hands on the sick, and they shall recover" (Mark 16:17–18).

"For verily I say unto you, that whosoever shall say unto this mountain, be you removed, and be you cast into the sea; and shall not doubt in his heart, but shall believe that those things which he says shall come to pass; he shall have whatsoever he says" (Mark 11:23).

4. *Patience.* Colossians 1:10–11 says "that all of you might walk worthy of the Lord unto all pleasing, being fruitful in every good work, and increasing in the knowledge of God; Strengthened with all might, according to his glorious power, unto all patience and longsuffering with joyfulness." James 1:3–4 says, "knowing this, that the trying of your faith works patience. But let patience have her perfect work, that all of you may be perfect and entire, lacking nothing." And Colossian's 3:12–13, "Put on therefore, as the elect of God, holy and beloved, bowels of mercies, kindness, humbleness of mind, meekness,

longsuffering; Forbearing one another, and forgiving one another, if any man have a quarrel against any: even as Christ forgave you, so also do all of you."

This same *love* becomes the *radio* of our heart, which produces *praise, worship, faith, adoration, confession, and thanksgiving.*

STEP 10

Chimney: Developing a Relationship with God

The chimney plays a most important role for the fireplace because it takes away the caustic elements and a portion of the fragrance of what being burned to the outside world so while the one on the inside may enjoy the warmth of the fire and suffers not the smoke. Those who may be walking about on the outside may smell the aroma of that being burned; so, too, is prayer which is the vehicle by which we send up our offering unto God. Pray brings us closer into the love of God and from that issue forth the warmth, comfort and transformation from what was toxic to our inner man to that of one knowing that it is not by his might, craftiness or his meekness but by the will of God. First Peter 3:12 states, "For the eyes of the Lord are over the righteous, and his ears are open unto their prayers: but the face of the Lord is against them that do evil."

Through prayer, faith is established and increased; therefore, it brings forth praise, worship, adoration, confession, and thanksgiving which radiate from every portion of your being. Just as there is an order to building a house so, too, God has an order by which his temple is to be built. Second Peter 1:4–10 says,

Whereby are given unto us exceeding great and precious promises: that by these ye might be partakers of the divine nature, having escaped the corruption that is in the world through lust. And beside this, giving all diligence, add to your faith virtue; and to virtue knowledge; And to knowledge willful restrain; and to willful restrain patience; and to patience godliness; And to godliness brotherly kindness; and to brotherly kindness love. For if these things be in you, and abound, they make you that you shall neither be barren nor unfruitful in the knowledge of our Lord Jesus Christ. But he that lacks these things is blind, and cannot see far off, and has forgotten that he was purged from his old sins. Wherefore the rather, brethren, give diligence to make your calling and election sure: for if ye do these things, ye shall never fall.

Know ye not that ye are the temple of God, and that the Spirit of God dwells in you? If any man defile the temple of God, him shall God destroy; for the temple of God is holy, which temple ye are. (1 Corinthians 3:16–17).

When our eyes of understanding become clear we recognize what is Christ's hope for us and the greatness of the gift that he has given unto us now and forever for those who are his children. We learn our duty towards Father, Son and the Holy Spirit. Romans 12:1–2 says,

I plead to you therefore, brethren, by the mercies of God, that ye present your bodies a living sacrifice, holy, acceptable unto God, which is your reasonable service. And be not conformed to this world: but be ye transformed by the renewing of your mind, that ye may prove what is that good, and acceptable, and perfect, will of God.

When our eyes of understanding become clear, we understand the important of our service unto the Lord. Jesus said that if any man believes in him that he would come and dwell with him (John 14:23, paraphrase). Also, in John 15:15–16, Jesus said,

> Henceforth I call you not servants; for the servant knows not what his lord does: but I have called you friends; for all things that I have heard of my Father I have made known unto you. Ye have not chosen me, but I have chosen you, and ordained you, that you should go and bring forth fruit, and that your fruit should remain: that whatsoever ye shall ask of the Father in my name, he may give it you.

STEP 11

Light: Life in Jesus Christ

When darkness is all around, you cannot see the beauty of the house or how to move within the house until light has been brought to bear. Everyone seeks to have a long life of joy, peace, and love without struggle, but life is constant movement toward perfection and not knowing how to obtain it becomes a struggle that at times is more than one can bear. So, too, in our life (spiritual), without light (understanding of who God is), it becomes difficult to move. So we struggle to get things done or we put things off until a new day arises. We live life as though beating at air, we walk in spiritual darkness, having no idea of God's love for us or his righteousness when that new day arise. First John 1:5–10 says,

> This then is the message which we have heard of him, and declare unto you, that God is light, and in him is no darkness at all. If we say that we have fellowship with him, and walk-in darkness, we lie, and do not the truth: But if we walk in the light, as he is in the light, we have fellowship one with another, and the blood of Jesus Christ his Son cleanses us from all sin. If we say that we have no sin, we deceive ourselves, and the truth is not in us. If we confess our sins, he is faithful and

just to forgive us our sins, and to cleanse us from all unrighteousness. If we say that we have not sinned, we make him a liar, and his word is not in us.

In order to stay in fellowship with God, we must "present our bodies as a living sacrifice, holy, acceptable unto God, which is our reasonable service (while we were yet sinners Jesus Christ gave his life for us) and be not conformed to this world but be ye transformed by the renewing of your mind, that you may prove what is good, acceptable and the prefect will of God" (Roman 12:1–2).

That you may, let your light so shine before men, that they may see your good works, and glorify your Father which is in heaven. "Recompense to no man evil for evil. Provide things honest in the sight of all men" (Matthew 5:16). "If it be possible, as much as lies in you, live peaceably with all men" (Romans 12:17–18). "That all of you may be blameless and harmless, the sons of God, without rebuke, in the midst of a crooked and perverse nation, among whom all of you shine as lights in the world" (Philippians 2:15).

STEP 12

Table: Fruits of the Spirit

There are few places within the house that will bring the family together like assembling around the dining table to eat. The dining table brings an air of unity and friendship and a demonstration of love for the food and the people that are there. The Holy Spirit is that table in which the fruits of love, joy, peace, longsuffering, gentleness, goodness, and faith are served, and when consumed, they bring forth more fruit in good works. Psalms 1 says,

> Blessed is the man that walks not in the counsel of the ungodly, nor stands in the way of sinners, nor sits in the seat of the scornful. But his delight is in the law of the Lord; and in his law does he meditate day and night. And he shall be like a tree planted by the rivers of water, that brings forth his fruit in his season; his leaf also shall not wither; and whatsoever he does shall prosper. The ungodly are not so: but are like the chaff which the wind drives away. Therefore, the ungodly shall not stand in the judgment, nor sinners in the congregation of the righteous. For the Lord knows the way of the righteous: but the way of the ungodly shall perish.

When we were free from righteousness, we did things by our own standards and now we are ashamed, because we have been freed from sin and become servant of God, we have fruits (works) of holiness and the end toward an everlasting life. Strengthened with all might, according to his glorious power, unto all patience and longsuffering with joyfulness (Romans 6:22–23, paraphrased; Colossians 1:11). The atmosphere in the house is joyous because of the surety of the people within and in that sense, the Holy Spirit brings that surety of us with God and the peace produces patience and patient, longsuffering, from which a life is reflective of the goodness and gentleness that the Lord has shown unto us.

STEP 13

Chair: Meekness

The chairs around the dining room table are never thought to be an important item, but if chairs that are too large, they tend to overpower the table and the person sitting in the chairs; or if the chairs are too small, they tend to understate the position of the person who is sitting in it. Too large, too close, too small, and too far away, but when the chairs conform to the atmosphere of the room the size of the chairs will always fit. Meekness is our chairs, which offer peace and rest to the weary, and it does not present itself more highly than it should but rather covers itself in a servant position. Romans 12:2 states that "be not conformed to this world: but be all of you transformed by the renewing of your mind, that all of you may prove what is that good, and acceptable, and perfect, will of God."

"But in your hearts revere Christ as Lord. Always be prepared to give an answer to everyone who asks you to give the reason for the hope that you have. But do this with gentleness and respect" (1 Peter 3:15, New International Version). Therefore, whatever situation you find yourself in you are satisfied in knowing that the lord is with you.

STEP 14

Bed: Joy

The bed is another important piece of furniture within the house. If it doesn't fit in length and width or in softness and firmness, then it doesn't provide for a rejuvenating rest from all the worry and cares of the world. When the bed is right, there is always joy of wakening and seeing a new day and what it will present and knowing that you are ready to meet the challenges of the day. Joy is the happiness that come with the confident in knowing who you are, where you going and what you are doing. This surety is what we most desire (to know that God is with us), for the word says in Isaiah 55:6, "Seek ye the Lord while he may be found, call upon him while he is near."

"Behold, I stand at the door and knock. If anyone hears My voice and opens the door [of his heart], I will come in to him and dine with him [true fellowship] and he with Me" (Revelations 3:20).

In this surety, we have a oneness with Lord and a promise of help in the times of trouble.

> Be careful for nothing; but in everything by prayer and supplication with thanksgiving let your requests be made known unto God. And the peace of God, which passes all understanding, shall keep your hearts and minds through Christ Jesus. Finally, brethren,

whatsoever things are true, whatsoever things are honest, whatsoever things are just, whatsoever things are pure, whatsoever things are lovely, whatsoever things are of good report; if there be any virtue, and if there be any praise, think on these things. Those things, which you have both learned, and received, and heard, and seen in me, do: and the God of peace shall be with you. (Philippians 4:6–9)

It is this surety that brings the strength to walk where one can't see, to stand still in the face of the storms of life and truly rely on the greater one that is in you than all the things in the world.

STEP 15

Couch: Gentleness

The couch is another piece of furniture that occupies a center portion of the house, for it is where you come after a long day to relax from the stress and strain of the day. The couch demands nothing from you except that you sit and receive the gentle caress of comfort. Here we do a review of the day's successes and failures, renewing the determination in the things that produce success and seeking help with the things that fell. What then is the couch of man's spirit? It is the relationship with God. Again Revelation 3:20 says, "Behold, I stand at the door, and knock: if any man hears my voice, and open the door, I will come in to him, and will sup with him, and he with me." This is a relationship that is created by love and that love gave a sacrifice that no other could ever give. That sacrifice was Jesus, and he took not a position of high estate but one of gentleness, humility, and lowliness. Jesus being that perfect sacrifice demonstrated how to establish a relationship with the father through prayer.

Prayer has many elements to it, one of faith, worship, thanksgiving, confession, adoration, and praise, and just like the couch, prayer is central and vital in the relationship with the Father through Christ Jesus. Prayer demonstrates that we believe in God (the Father), Jesus Christ (his atoning sacrifice), the Holy Spirit which was his gift to us through which we are connected with God through the Son. Just as we find comfort in just the right spot in our couch, the same comfort and overwhelming joy come from the conversations we have in prayer with our Lord and Savior. Through prayer, revelations are given and the weak places in our lives are made strong and our faith in God is made surer. You learn the value of yourself in God, God in you and the living a servant life.

Jesus said in John 15:15, "Henceforth I call you not servants; for the servant knoweth not what his lord doeth: but I have called you friend; for all things that I gave heard of my Father I have made know unto you." So, our relationship is one of love and not of servitude.

STEP 16

TV: Word of God

The TV could be our best friend or our worst enemy because it brings us pictures and views from around the world or what is happening in our own little area. The TV shows the cause and effect through the eyes of the one who is reporting on the event. If the couch equals to prayer, then the Word of God is our TV because it shows or manifest what the Word of God has said. The reading of God's word from Genesis to Revelations gives a picture of what was said and what was manifested for the completion of the word. God's word is just as reflective then as it is now. God said in the book of Genesis concerning creation, "Let There Be," and whatsoever stated to be preform was made to appear.

The power of God's word brings into being just what he had said but without faith in God there can be no understanding of him and the visual effects he has on our lives. Hebrews 11:6 says, "But without faith it is impossible to please him: for he that comes to God must believe that he is, and that he is a rewarder of them that diligently seek him," seeing what he has said became real in us and around us. Isaiah 55:11 says that his word will proceed from his mouth and it will not return unto him void, but it will accomplish that which was said and it shall prosper in the thing whereto he sent it. Jesus says in Matthew 7:11 that "if you then being evil, know how to give good gifts to your children, how much more will your Father who is in heaven give good things to those who ask Him!"

> Behold, what manner of love the Father has bestowed upon us, that we should be called the sons of God: therefore, the world knows us not, because it knew him not. Beloved, now are we the sons of God, and it does not yet appear what we shall be: but we know that, when he shall appear, we shall be like him; for we shall see him as he is. (1 John 3:1–2)

John 3:16 says, "For God so loved the world that He gave Him only begotten Son, that who-soever believes in Him should not perish but have but have everlasting life." In this ever-changing world God has said through his word that he would always be a constant, standing when everything else falls.

STEP 17

Yard: Righteousness

The beauty of a house is first presented by the beautification of the yard. The presentation of the flowers, shrugs and grass really set the look of the house from the outside. The yard is the first welcome mat to the house before you reach the front door. A yard in disrepair can and will affect how one view the whole house. The yard, in almost all cases, will reflect the inner condition of the house and so, too, is the heart of man.

Jesus, in Luke 8:4–15, taught the disciples and the people that gather around this parable about the Sower and the seed. He said that

> a Sower went out to sow his seed and as he did it some fell by the wayside [ground that wasn't prepared to receive the seed], the birds came an ate the seeds or was walk upon as sowing continued. There were some seeds that fell among rocks and when they grew up the died from a lack water, some fell among thorns; when the seeds and thorns grew up the thorns overpowered the seed so that they couldn't produce. There were seeds that did fall on the ground that was prepared for them and when the came up, they grew and produce much fruit.

The disciples came to Jesus after his teaching and ask what type of parable it was. Jesus said unto them it is needful for you the know the mysteries of the kingdom of God, "(because they were that good ground)", but to the others in the parables; that seeing that they may not see and hearing they might not understand.

Jesus goes on to explain the parable:

1. Those that are by the wayside are those that hear the word; then the devil comes and takes the word out of their hearts before belief come and they be saved.

   John 3: 15–17 says, "That whosoever believes in him should not perish, but have eternal life. For God so loved the world, that he gave his only begotten Son, that whosoever believes in him should not perish, but have everlasting life. For God sent not his Son into the world to condemn the world; but that the world through him might be saved."

2. Those that were rocky when they heard the word receive it with joy but because they had no understanding, believe for a while but return to their old ways in due time.

   "That Christ may dwell in your hearts by faith; that you, being rooted and grounded in love, may be able to comprehend with all saints what is the breadth, and length, and depth, and height, and to know the love of Christ, which passes knowledge, that you might be filled with all the fullness of God" (Ephesians 3:17–19).

3. Those that fell among the thorns are they which heard they word, received, and went forth to do, but did not bring any work to completions because of still desiring the riches and pleasures of life.

   "And the cares of this world, and the deceitfulness of riches, and the lusts of other things entering in, choke the word, and it becomes unfruitful" (Mark 4:19).

4. Those that fell on good ground are they that after hearing, received the word with honest and sincere heart, kept the word, and manifested the result of the word with patience.

"Blessed is the man that walks not in the counsel of the ungodly, nor stands in the way of sinners, nor sits in the seat of the scornful. But his delight is in the law of the Lord; and in his law does he meditate day and night. And he shall be like a tree planted by the rivers of water, that brings forth his fruit in his season; his leaf also shall not wither; and whatsoever he does shall prosper" (Psalms 1:1–3). The heart of man manifests the love of God and by this we know that we are children of God when we love the children of God and kept his commandments.

STEP 18

Insurance: The Armor of God

Now that the house and yard construction is completed and moving in is due. One of the concerns is having help replacing or repairing the house in the case of lost or damage. The price of the insurance could be very high due to the place where it is built or the types of coverage, such as flood-, earthquake-, or fire-prone areas. Unlike the insurance on a physical house which is sought after the house is built. The price for the insurance of the spiritual house of God has already been paid an is activated with the very moment the decision is made.

How can this be?

1. *Love*

For God so loved the world, that he gave his only begotten Son, that whosoever believes in him should not perish, but have everlasting life. (John 3:16)

This is my commandment, That ye love one another, as I have loved you. Greater love has no man than this, that a man lay down his life for his friends. Ye are my friends, if ye do whatsoever I command you. Henceforth I call you not servants;

for the servant knows not what his lord does: but I have called you friends; for all things that I have heard of my Father I have made known unto you. (John 15:12–15)

2. *Hearing of the Word*

For whosoever shall call upon the name of the Lord shall be saved. How then shall they call on him in whom they have not believed? and how shall they believe in him of whom they have not heard? and how shall they hear without a preacher? And how shall they preach, except they be sent? (Romans 10:13–15a)

Ask, and it shall be given you; seek, and you shall find; knock, and it shall be opened unto you: For every one that asks receives; and he that seeks finds; and to him that knocks it shall be opened. (Matthew 7:7–8)

3. *Faith*

Now faith is the substance of things hoped for, the evidence of things not seen. (Hebrew 11:1)

So then faith comes by hearing, and hearing by the word of God. (Romans 10:17)

That if you shall confess with your mouth the Lord Jesus, and shall believe in your heart that God has raised him from the dead, you shall be saved. For with the heart man believes untorighteousness; and with the mouth confession is made unto salvation. (Romans 10:9–10)

4. *Holy Spirit*

But you shall receive power, after that the Holy Spirit has come upon you. (Acts 1:8a)

For to one is given by the Spirit the word of wisdom; to another the word of knowledge by the same Spirit; To another faith by the same Spirit; to another the gifts of healing by the same Spirit; To another the working of miracles; to another prophecy; to another discerning of spirits; to another divers kinds of tongues; to another the interpretation of tongues: But all these works that one and the very same Spirit, dividing to every man severally as he will. (1 Corinthians 12:8–11)

5. *Power*

And these signs shall follow them that believe; In my name shall they cast out devils; they shall speak with new tongues; They shall take up serpents; and if they drink any deadly thing, it shall not hurt them; they shall lay hands on the sick, and they shall recover. (Mark 16:17–18)

Jesus answered and said unto them, Verily I say unto you, if you have faith, and doubt not, all of you shall not only do this which is done to the fig tree, but also if all of you shall say unto this mountain, Be you removed, and be you cast into the sea; it shall be done. (Matthew 21:21)

6. *Oneness with God*

Abide in me, and I in you. As the branch cannot bear fruit of itself, except it abide in the vine; no more can ye, except ye abide in me. I am the vine, ye are the branches: He that abides in me, and I in him, the same brings forth much fruit: for without me ye can do nothing. Ye have not chosen me, but I have chosen you, and ordained you, that ye should go and bring forth fruit, and that your fruit should remain: that whatsoever ye shall ask of the Father in my name, he may give it you. (John 15:4–5, 16)

I beseech you therefore, brethren, by the mercies of God, that ye present your bodies a living sacrifice, holy and expectable unto God, which is your reasonable service. And be not conformed to this world: but be ye transformed by the renewing of your mind, that ye may prove what is that good, and acceptable, and perfect, will of God. (Romans 12:1–2)

Know ye not that you are the temple of God, and that the Spirit of God dwells in you? (1 Corinthians 3:16)

Wherefore take unto you the whole armour of God, that you may be able to withstand in the evil day, and having done all, to stand. Stand therefore, having your loins girt about with truth, and having on the breastplate of righteousness; And your feet shod with the preparation of the gospel of peace; Above all, taking the shield of faith, wherewith you shall be able to quench all the fiery darts of the wicked. And take the helmet of salvation, and the sword of the Spirit, which is the word) of God: Praying always with all prayer and supplication in the Spirit, and watching thereunto with all perseverance and supplication for all saints. (Ephesians 6:13–18)

This house of the Lord is never done for there is always things to be added and things to improve upon. Matthew 7:7–11 says,

Ask, and it shall be given you; seek, and you shall find; knock, and it shall be opened unto you: For every one that asks receives; and he that seeks finds; and to him that knocks it shall be opened. Or what man is there of you, whom if his son ask bread, will he give him a stone? Or if he ask a fish, will he give him a serpent? If all of you then, being evil, know how to give good gifts unto your children, how much more shall your Father which is in heaven give good things to them that ask him?

So the more we give unto the Father (God), the more he will allow you to view what he has already given unto you.

ABOUT THE AUTHOR

Calvin Taylor is a father of three grown children who all have strong relationship with God. He is a proud veteran from the United States Army, ordained deacon and teacher, a member of Freedom Church International of Pell city Alabama. Early on in his life he always found himself asking questions about God that was beyond his age and as he grew, he learned that the most important thing a person who called himself a Christian must have is a relationship with God. He is still that child asking question and God keep answering so that there will be no excuse when he come.